How to Be a Juggler

A RINGLING BROS. AND BARNUM & BAILEY BOOK

HOW TO BE A JUGGLER

Charles R. Meyer

DAVID McKAY COMPANY, INC.
NEW YORK

COPYRIGHT © 1977 by Charles R. Meyer and Ringling Bros.-Barnum & Bailey Combined Shows, Inc.

Library of Congress Cataloging in Publication Data

Meyer, Charles Robert, 1926-
How to be a juggler.

(A Ringling Brothers and Barnum & Bailey book)
SUMMARY: Describes how to become a juggler and instructs the novice in the manipulation of all kinds of objects.
1. Jugglers and juggling—Juvenile literature.
[1. Jugglers and juggling] I. Title.
GV1548.M49   793.8   77-10664
ISBN 0-679-20407-5

10 9 8 7 6 5 4 3 2 1

MANUFACTURED IN THE UNITED STATES OF AMERICA

DESIGN: H. ROBERTS

To all the Ringling Bros. and Barnum & Bailey
Circus jugglers past, present, and future,
who really wrote this book by proxy

Contents

Introduction

THE ART OF juggling is far from new. History tells us there were jugglers many centuries before the first circus.

What sort of objects have jugglers used? They include fiery hoops, pebbles, plates, umbrellas, billiard cues, bottles, lamps, washing tubs, hats, balls, candlesticks, bowling pins, knives, stones, swords, cigars, and limbs from trees. The list of props employed by ancient and modern jugglers is seemingly endless, limited only by the imagination and skill of the performers.

After you have learned the basic techniques of juggling, perhaps you will be able to add something spectacular and entirely different to your juggling routine. If you try hard and practice enough, you can learn tricks that will make your audience gasp and burst into applause.

1

An early circus strong-man juggler (c. 1880).

To become as expert as a professional circus juggler, you will have to combine patience with hours of practice. Keeping three balls or clubs in the air at the same time may appear to be almost impossible. But remember to keep one thing in mind: After a great deal of effort and concentration on your part, juggling will suddenly become easy. Try it and see.

The incomparable Picaso, the greatest, fastest juggler
the world has ever known.

How to Start Juggling

WE'LL BEGIN WITH the ABCs of juggling. They are really no harder than the basic techniques of roller skating, spinning a Yo-Yo, or riding a bicycle. Although you will probably make mistakes and find things slightly difficult in the beginning, juggling skills become easy once you know how they work. Once you understand and are able to perform a two-ball and a three-ball cascade, you will be able to develop your own juggling routines.

The art of circus juggling begins when you pick up such objects as balls and make them perform an aerial dance.

What sort of balls are best? Tennis balls are the most commonly available. But lacrosse balls are even better. Rubber balls, about two and one-half inches in diameter, baseballs, sponge balls, golf balls, and handballs can be used also. Plastic bowl-

Ringling Bros. and Barnum & Bailey clown Bob Boasi teaches juggling techniques to Charles R. Meyer, Jr.

Ringling Bros. and Barnum & Bailey circus jugglers, 1906.

ing pins, the kind that are found in department store toy counters, hula hoops, empty or full soda cans, and even refrigerated oranges are other possibilities. Start with whatever objects are the most inexpensive and handiest.

As you become more expert at juggling, you will discover that the surface of the balls is an important factor. A highly polished billiard ball may become slippery from perspiration and slip through your fingers; a fuzzy-surfaced ball absorbs moisture and causes the palms of your hands to become too dry for a really firm grip. If you have a choice, choose balls with moderately rough and unvarnished surfaces. However, the type of ball you begin with doesn't really make a great difference.

First clench and open your hands several times. Make a fist and stretch out your fingers. Limber up like a pitcher on the mound or a track star preparing for a race. You must be completely at ease and relaxed when you are juggling.

Stand in front of a wall with your hands in front of your waist, palms up. Take a ball and throw it from one hand to the other in a graceful arc no higher than the level of your eyes or forehead. Don't raise your hands to catch the ball. Keep both hands in front of your waist and allow the ball to come to you. Stay at the same distance from the wall without moving your feet.

The ball should be "popped," or flipped, out of the palm of your hand so that it hangs momentarily motionless at the top of its flight, without spinning sideways. It should move in a parallel plane in front

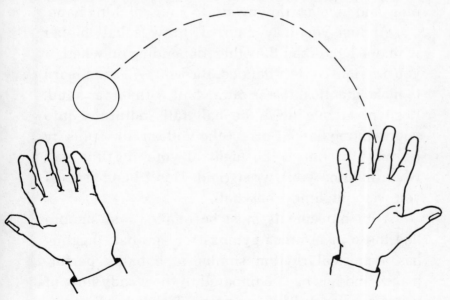

of your body so that you won't have to reach with the other hand to catch it. Don't be surprised if your left hand is weaker than your right. In the beginning it's difficult to keep the ball at approximately the same height in successive throws. Wind a thin strip of colored tape around the ball so that you can easily see and correct any spins. One well-known juggling instructor tells his students to imagine holding a picture frame with their two hands at its bottom corners. The ball should rise to a peak in front of the juggler's forehead at the top of the frame. The ball should never stray out of the frame! Practice the exercise until your left and right hands automatically throw the ball just hard enough to reach your forehead, hang motionless without spinning, and then arc downward to your catching hand.

At first you may tend to throw a ball higher with one hand than the other, depending on whether you are right- or left-handed. But you will soon learn to make identical tosses of the ball with either hand. Keep practicing until the ball falls naturally into your waiting hand. Correct the undesirable spins by learning to control the flight of your juggling ball while holding your wrist rigid. Don't bend it as if you were pitching a baseball.

Your movements must be relaxed and smooth like those of a circus gymnast or acrobat. Juggling has a musical rhythm similar to a ballet performance and has been compared to the steady flow of water in a brook. This is a particularly good descrip-

Francis Brunn, Ringling Bros. and Barnum & Bailey Circus, 1950.

tion of cascade juggling, in which objects are thrown into the air from an inside position closer to the center of your own body, then allowed to descend into the juggler's hands from the outside.

Basically, juggling with balls is merely a matter of tossing and catching them according to a pattern. The palms and fingers of your hands should flip the balls upward at precisely the right time. Gravity causes the balls to descend, and the process can be repeated with variations. The technique you are about to learn has been described as "teaching the balls to dance." The juggling movements you use with a single ball are exactly the same as those you will use with three or more balls.

Two-Ball Juggling

Now THAT YOU know a little about juggling, you should be more particular about your choice of juggling balls. The weight of the ball, its size, and its surface texture are important when you attempt more complicated juggling tricks. You should obtain a good set of basic juggler's tools—three solid rubber or lacrosse balls. Be sure you can comfortably and easily hold two of them in either your left or right hand.

Don't go to a great amount of trouble if the exact balls you want are not stocked in your neighborhood sporting-goods or toy store. Temporarily, tennis balls will do the job, although they are not suitable for advanced tricks. But no matter what kind of balls you choose, you should mark them with a colored grease crayon so that you can readily tell one from another while they are flying

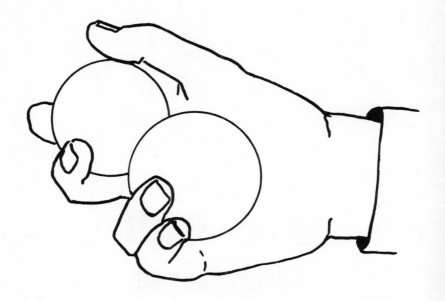

through the air. The material on the outside of the balls should be washable because they will certainly bounce into dusty corners and under furniture if you miss a catch.

First, place two balls in your right hand (or in your left, if you are left-handed). One ball should rest in the cup of your palm, grasped by your little and third fingers; the other ball should be lightly gripped by your thumb and index and middle fingers. "Pop," or flip, the outside or "fingertip," ball from one hand to the other in a graceful arc. Remember, the maximum height of the ball should not exceed the level of your eyes or forehead. Don't raise your hands to catch the ball. Keep both of your hands in front of your waist, as if you were carrying a tray of dishes, and let the ball descend. Don't lift your hand to catch it.

Practice this in front of a bed or couch so you

won't waste energy chasing the ball when you miss. Try to stand in one place and not walk forward, chasing the balls as you juggle. Throw the balls with your right hand, and then back again with your left hand, until the path of the ball through the air in either case is similar.

When you have to reach outward or inward from your normal hand position to catch the ball, correct your throw so that the ball hangs almost motionless in front of your eyes at the top of the arc before it falls into your waiting hand.

Place a third ball in your left hand and repeat the practice. Throw the fingertip ball from right to left, left to right, right to left; learn to catch the thrown ball on your fingertips with either hand. Continue this exercise for several days until you are just as expert with your left hand as your right hand, or until you can complete at least a dozen throws without missing. It is extremely important that you should not have to step forward or backward to make a catch. When you have learned to do this, you will be ready for another important juggling exercise.

Place two balls in your right hand. Put your left hand behind your back or in your pocket. With the right hand only, palm up, toss the fingertip ball, or the ball farthest from your body, up to a height of two feet above your head. As it begins to descend, move your hand slightly to the right. Then toss the other ball up to the identical height. Shift your hand slightly to the left again to catch the original ball on

your fingertips in the same position from which it was originally thrown. Move your hand to the right again and repeat.

A variation of this exercise is to toss the first ball upward and slightly to the right. While the ball is in the air, move your hand in a small clockwise circle so that you can catch the ball when your hand is to the right side of the circle. Repeat the process with your left hand. The ball will actually be moving in a large circular path while your hand duplicates the motion in a smaller but similar rotation. Try this with two balls. Keep a constant pattern of balls rotating in the air.

What are you learning? Balance, coordination, rhythm, and hand manipulation—the basic talents of a professional circus juggler.

Now put your right hand behind your back or in your pocket. Start the ball dancing with your left hand. It will be difficult in the beginning.

Try juggling the balls with your right hand. You will gradually be able to perform with either hand. Transfer the balls from your right to your left hand without breaking the tempo or dropping a ball. All you have to do is throw a ball from one cupped palm to the other, while the fingertip ball is in the air. You should allow the ball in your cupped palm to roll down onto your fingertips before you throw it upward. Now you are beginning to perform like a professional juggler.

Here are some fundamental rules that may help

Hugh Zuniga, instructor and performer at Circus World in Haines City, Florida, teaches the author's son the basics of ball juggling.

when you run into difficulties while you're learning to juggle:

1. Practice in front of a bed or a sofa to eliminate chasing around after balls when they collide in mid-air or when you miss a catch.

2. There is no need to concentrate on each ball. Watch the entire area, or frame, in which the balls are doing their aerial dance. If you keep your hands in the proper position, the "catching" part of the juggling operation will take care of itself.

3. Relax. Take things slowly and rhythmically.

A juggler who is tense and "uptight" is unable to perform well.

4. Although experts argue about the height and curve of the balls in the air, you should keep them at eye or forehead levels, except for specific tricks and exercises. In the beginning, stick to the standard height. Later on, after you become an expert, you can change things to suit your own physical abilities and talents.

5. Remember to keep your elbows close to your body and your hands level in front of your waist, as if you were carrying a tray of dishes. Keep your arm and wrist motions to a minimum when you throw the balls. If you are forced to step forward or backward to make a catch, correct your next throw so you can juggle the balls while standing in one spot.

6. Don't try to grip the balls tightly when you make a catch. Hold them loosely and lightly so they can be propelled back into the air with a minimum of muscular effort.

7. Expect to make plenty of mistakes. Don't be discouraged if it takes time to make one hand work just as well as the other.

Remember that juggling takes practice, concentration, and more practice . . . until the techniques become easy. No amount of mere reading will ever make the balls dance in the air. If you doubt it, just ask any Ringling Bros. and Barnum & Bailey Circus juggler.

The Three-Ball Cascade

YOU MAY BE able to learn the fundamentals of juggling with the greatest of ease. If so, you are exceptionally lucky. Most people must grit their teeth, endure their mistakes, and develop juggling techniques through patience and determination.

When you are thoroughly at ease with the two-ball exercises described in the previous chapter, you are ready to attempt the three-ball cascade, or fountain juggling. Briefly, the balls ascend from the central area in front of your body and descend from the outside in a circular path, like water cascading from a fountain. Don't expect this juggling exercise to be easy. It separates the part-time amateur from the serious student who is apt to become as good as a professional circus juggler.

Juggling three balls with ease in a symmetrical path is the first phase of being a comedian-enter-

19

Hugh Zuniga teaches students the fundamentals of ball juggling.

tainer. It can be likened to climbing a steep ravine in preparation for scaling a high mountain. Once you have mastered the three-ball cascade, you are on your way toward becoming a star. The rest of the journey—with all the fancy tricks and decorative touches—will be at your fingertips if you want to juggle your way into the limelight.

Keep in mind that the three balls you juggle in a cascade pattern should *never* pass in front or in back of each other. They must always move above, below, or next to each other, at identical distances from your body. Just as you juggled two balls, you must imagine that the three balls are confined within a picture frame. They should travel from the mid-section of the bottom of the frame up to its top corners and back down again.

Spain's sensational juggler Picaso performs with hands—and mouth!

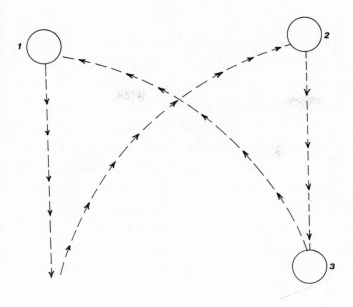

Place two balls in your right hand and a third ball in your left. Throw the fingertip ball (in your right hand) from right to left. It should rise in the air and pass across your eyes or forehead before it starts to fall toward your waiting left hand. As it falls, *but before it lands,* move your left hand slightly to the right and flip the second ball upward to the right, *inside the path of the first ball,* before you move it back to catch the first ball. Similarly, as the second ball descends, but before it reaches your right hand, move your right hand slightly to the left and throw the third ball *underneath* the second ball. Then return your hand to its original position in order to catch the second ball. This may sound simple in print. In practice, you will promptly run into trouble when two balls collide in the air.

How can you avoid collisions? One method is to throw the first ball slightly wide of your left hand *toward the outside of your body.* Another system is to move your hands farther apart and closer together in an independent rhythm, one after the other, to match the "throw" and "catch" pattern.

Try both methods and use whichever works best for you. You may want to combine elements of both. If not, you may have to concentrate very hard (and chase a great many balls dropped onto the floor) until the three-ball cascade becomes almost automatic and easy to perform for extended lengths of time.

Now you are a juggler—almost! Now you can proudly display your technique and perform before your family and friends. But now is also the time when you should consider whether you want your juggling to be a pure accomplishment by itself or part of an entertainer's act. Perhaps, like top show-business comedians of yesteryear—W. C. Fields, Fred Allen, and Jimmy Savo, for instance—you might want to use your juggling as part of an act, rather than the focus of an entire performance. Or perhaps like the king of all the jugglers in circus history, Enrico Rastelli, you'll want to become the next "best juggler on earth."

You could learn four-, five-, six-, and even seven-ball juggling through years of practice, rigid discipline, and concentration. You might mix juggling objects such as rings, clubs, bottles, hats, ice

Shelly Spivey, a white face clown at Circus World, learns juggling techniques at Clown College.

cubes, plates, or disks. Juggling is sometimes a part of a magician's routine at school shows or the center act of the Ringling Bros. and Barnum & Bailey Circus extravaganza. It is also used to divert the audience's attention while circus crews are setting up props. Or it can be part of a balancing or trapeze act. Juggling might simply be a pleasurable hobby that you learn entirely for fun. The choice is yours.

Extend Your Juggling Horizons

Now THAT YOU are able to perform three-ball cascade juggling without a great deal of difficulty, you can try "showering," a trick in which the path of the balls gives the appearance of a circular or oval figure. One ball follows the other without crossing it. First try this with two balls.

Place both balls in your right hand and throw the fingertip ball, the one farthest from your body, from right to left, making a half circle upward and slightly inward, about two feet high. The left hand receiving the ball should be approximately eighteen inches from the right hand and slightly higher. As soon as the fingertip ball leaves your right hand, let the ball cupped in your palm slide down to your fingertips. Throw it from side to side across your body. Catch the first ball in your left hand and immediately send it back toward the right hand with

The Fantastic Fudi.

a straight, short, and slightly downward throw. Catch the second ball in your left hand and flip it back toward the right in exactly the same manner. But start the first ball on the arc of its return journey for the next cycle before the second ball arrives in your right hand.

Showering balls makes a pretty picture for your audience, and it isn't as hard as it looks. You will soon be able to mix the "cascade" and "shower" forms of juggling by breaking the rhythm of one and swinging into the other without dropping a ball.

To shower three balls, start with two in your right hand and one in your left. Using the same pattern as the two-ball shower, pop the fingertip ball from your right hand slightly higher than the ones following. Start the second ball while the first is in the air. While they are both aloft, quickly transfer the third ball from left to right with a straight-line throw. As the first ball is caught in your left hand, toss the ball entering your right hand.

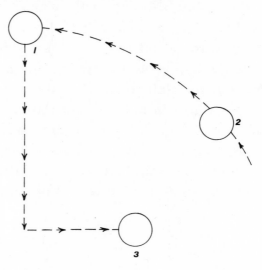

Students at Clown College, Venice, Florida.

Until now, you have been standing in one spot with your hands in front of your waist, concentrating on the juggling balls. Now that you have mastered those techniques, repeat them while walking across a room or down a street. Try juggling the balls while twirling a hula hoop around your thighs. Or put on a Santa Claus suit and juggle three Christmas-tree balls. You might also dress yourself in a Ringling Bros. and Barnum & Bailey Circus clown outfit and juggle three ice cubes. Pretend to be horrified when they melt.

Cesar, shown here in his fantastic act, juggles while balancing on a slack wire.

One of the clowns in "The Greatest Show on Earth" juggles an apple, a pear, and an orange. Pretending to be hungry, he tries to take a bite out of the apple each time it passes near his mouth. He dodges backward in fright when he is almost hit by the orange. At the conclusion of his act, he throws the orange and the pear to people in the audience. Then he leans against a pole, contentedly eating his apple while the spectators laugh and applaud.

Another clown, dressed in a high silk hat, juggles three balls. But he makes one ball disappear into a hole in the top of his hat. After the clown runs around the ring in search of the missing ball, another clown yanks on the front of the first clown's jacket. The ball drops out of another hole in the front of his hat (which the original juggler controls by means of a string around the brim of that hat), and the juggling act is resumed.

Alex Dunai of Europe's famous Riding Dunai family.

Suspended only by her hair is Chrys Holt,
justly acclaimed juggling star.

Student at Clown College, Venice, Florida.

There are thousands of variations of juggling-comedy routines you can use once you have mastered the basic juggling skills.

If you learned the buffoonery of a clown, the dexterity of an acrobat, and the showmanship of a magician, you would be able to create a superlative circus act. If you blended those skills with the abilities of a juggler, management agents would be waiting in line to offer you contracts to perform all over the country. And with today's swiftly changing face of show business and television, you would be in a position to find a rewarding niche in whatever pattern tomorrow's circus entertainment may bring.

Start by practicing until you can juggle by instinct—without really thinking about it. All it requires on your part is practice, hour after hour, day after day, week after week. Try it and see.

31

Juggling with Hoops and Bowling Pins

IT IS GOING to be relatively easy for you to convert your three-ball juggling skills to the use of hoops and bowling pins. You have already accomplished the most difficult part of learning to juggle when you mastered the cascade and shower techniques with balls. Since the throwing and spinning of hoops might be described as a combination of ball and club juggling, we shall concentrate on the hoops first.

Start with three inexpensive hoops, or rings, available in toy stores. Purchase them in different colors, if possible. Your hoops should measure approximately twelve to fourteen inches around on the outside and between eight and nine inches around on the inside. If they are made of plastic, you might wrap them spiral-fashion, with different colored tapes to make them more attractive. You can

Bob Boasi, while still a student at Clown College.

The Marvelous Mairo presents amazing juggling and acrobatic feats on a single trapeze.

also use luminescent or phosphorescent reflective tapes, such as those used on bicycles to make them visible after dark. You can then have a spectacular act if you perform without lights.

Scientists tell us that every rotating body tends to maintain its motion. That law of physics includes juggling hoops. They will not collide in the air nearly as often as the balls you have used previously; since the hoops are narrow, they usually fly past each other without colliding. When they do hit, they do not cause a great problem because they don't bounce like balls.

To throw a hoop, grasp it in your palm with a firm finger grip. Snap your wrist so that the hoop spins upward. Make sure that the release position is slightly above your shoulder. To catch the hoop, simply bring your hand up underneath it and grasp it at its lowest position in flight.

Stand sideways to your audience so you can be seen more clearly. Practice outdoors, since you will be tossing your hoops much higher than juggling balls. Start by tossing and catching a single hoop over and over again until it spins evenly and does not quiver. Follow that exercise by tossing and catching two hoops at the same time, one in each hand, then try two hoops, one at a time, alternating your right and left hands.

Grip two hoops with one hand and practice tossing one of them without letting the other fall. To do this, throw the first hoop, using only your thumb

A busy lad is Cesar, wire-walking artist.

Chrys Holt *(left)* and juggling four balls *(right)*.

and index finger, while you grip the other hoop with your remaining fingers. You should be able to juggle two hoops in one hand after a few days of practice. To juggle three hoops follow the same principles you used for three-ball juggling, but throw the hoops higher so they have ample room to cross in the air. For variety, try throwing high and low tosses with the hoops.

Remember, always stand sideways to your audience so the full surface of the hoops is in view. You may also spin additional hoops on your legs or body in a hula-hoop action to make your performance more exciting.

The major difference between club juggling and the routines you have learned with balls and hoops is that the bowling pins "flip," or turn, in complete revolutions while in the air. Purchase plastic bowling pins from a toy store and practice complete flipover tosses with a single pin. Hold the pin so that your thumb is on one side and your fingers on the other in the center of the handle. In the beginning, throw one pin to a height slightly above your head. Later, you will be able to lower the toss.

To hold two pins in one hand, cross them slightly at the upper end of the handles. Your thumb and index finger should grip the one pin on the bottom (palm up) with the other three fingers gripping the second pin on top. This sounds much more complicated than it really is.

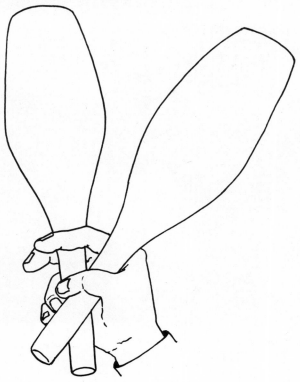

Charles R. Meyer, Jr.

Charles R. Meyer, Jr. juggling clubs.

In the beginning, make only one full rotation when you throw a pin. If you do not throw with enough force, the pin will not make a complete turn, and it will be difficult to catch. If you throw it too hard, you won't be able to grasp the handle and make a successful catch. When a pin is "overturned" or "underturned" you should compensate by giving it more or less wrist spin. Practice every day. Soon you will be an accomplished club juggler, ready to juggle a combination of pins and balls or pins and hoops. When you become truly expert, you will be able to handle soda cans, bottles, plates, disks, hats, and a variety of other props.

The basic juggling principles are the same no matter what sort of objects or combinations of objects you use. Success will depend upon your determination and day-after-day practice.

Juggling with Partners

THERE ARE A great number of flashy and entertaining tricks you can accomplish when you work with two or more jugglers. If you and another juggler stand side by side, one of you could function as the right hand and the other as the left hand. Thus, if you were performing a three-ball cascade, each of you would be using one hand. Or you might use your idle hand to do an independent balancing or spinning act just to make the routine fancier.

When you throw a pin to another juggler, lift it up in front of your body and swing it downward past your leg. Then bring the pin forward at arm's length and release it before straightening your arm. The weight of the pin will cause it to turn in the air. The proper amount of pressure, exerted by your thumb and fingers, is determined by practice and the distance between you and your juggling partner.

41

Above: Poland's famous Dubicki Troupe.
Below: Europe's Riding Dunai Family.

Instructor Hugo Zuniga *(right)* and students at the Clown College.

When your partner catches a pin in his left hand, he tosses it over to his right hand, and then follows the identical instructions above in throwing the pin back to you.

Start with one pin, then two, before you attempt three clubs for each juggler—with one member of the team setting the pace while the other simply follows the tempo. The usual system is for each juggler to throw two clubs to himself and the third to his partner as that club falls into his right hand; then two more and the next to his partner, etc. It is called "two between each throw." After that, you might try

throwing every other club falling into your right hand instead of every third. The different rhythm makes the act interesting.

Professional circus jugglers will tell you that from this start in double juggling any sort of formation work with any number of performers can be worked out. But without this basic training, team juggling can never be successful.

Don't worry or feel embarrassed about audience reactions when you first start performing in front of spectators. Remember to relax and concentrate entirely on your juggling.

Jokes for Circus Jugglers

THE FOLLOWING CIRCUS routines are intended to give you examples of the type of juggling act you might perform in order to make your audience laugh and applaud.

Inform them that you are about to juggle eight balls in a remarkable feat of dexterity. Build up the suspense by rummaging in a suitcase or a paper bag while pretending to have difficulty finding your props. Take out three balls with the number eight painted conspicuously on their sides and proceed to juggle.

Make what appears to be a book out of several pieces of paper and two pieces of cardboard. Print the words "How to Juggle" on the cardboard. Each time you miss a ball, open the book and tear out a page.

Keep a cap pistol tucked in your belt. Pull out

the gun and fire a volley whenever you drop a juggling ball.

Make a large sign that says "Genius at Work" on one side and "Failure at Work" on the other. Display one side or the other, depending on how the act is going. Have someone parade through the audience with the "Failure at Work" sign over their shoulder every time you drop a ball. Climax the act by firing your cap pistol at the clown carrying the sign.

Buy a pair of toy glasses with giant frames and put them on each time you drop a ball. As a variation on that theme, juggle ice cubes, but put the glasses on to help you discover where the ice cubes have gone when they finally melt and disappear.

In short, add comedy to your juggling act! It is said that one famous juggler practiced five hours daily for nearly two years until he learned to balance a billiard ball on top of a cue stick placed on his forehead. He held another stick in his left hand while he juggled three bowling pins in his right hand! But the act was a failure and he had to quit because nobody laughed! Remember that people come to the circus to forget their troubles, to be entertained, and to laugh. If you make your audience laugh, you will be a great success.

Great Circus Jugglers

THE WORD JUGGLER comes from the Latin *joculari,* to jest or joke. It has often been used to describe entertainers who achieve feats of balance while tossing and catching balls, plates, knives, clubs, and other objects.

The art of juggling was well known to the American Indian tribes long before Columbus discovered America. The Indians held contests with wooden sticks, stones, and balls. Old records indicate that Aztec jugglers at Emperor Montezuma's court in Mexico juggled with balls of solid rubber, and that the Chinook Indians of the Pacific Northwest were able to keep as many as seven pebbles rotating in the air. There were jugglers in ancient Rome, who specialized in juggling knives and who also performed with balls.

The Four Dunais make their American debut.

In the yellowed pages of an extremely old manuscript is an illustration of a large bear standing on its hind legs and juggling three knives. But no one knows if this really happened or if the picture stemmed from the artist's imagination. We do know that in the modern Russian circus a trainer named Valentin Filatov taught a bear to lie in a small cradle and juggle a flaming torch with its hind legs at a speed few humans could equal.

In the European circus of the nineteenth century, Asiatic jugglers were star attractions. Each contributed a specialized expertise that reflected his national upbringing. Young Chinese circus children still practice twirling wooden platters on sticks until they are skillful enough to use china or clay plates. Jugglers in India rotate four or more balls in the air at the same time.

The Oriental jugglers of the early circus introduced such feats as plate spinning and ribbon waving. A Western juggler named Hera used a routine in which he flipped nine candles into nine candlesticks with a mere twist of his wrist. An English lady juggler, Margot Edwards, showered five balls in the air while simultaneously riding bareback on a horse. How did she do it? Margot Edwards was a member of a circus family, and she had performed in the ring since she was four years old, and practice is what makes a circus performer perfect.

William Hazlitt once described an Indian juggler he saw at the English Olympic Theater in 1820:

Coming forward and seating himself on the ground in his white dress and tightened turban, the chief of the Indian jugglers begins by tossing up two brass balls, which is what any of us could do, and concludes by keeping up four at the same time, which is what none of us could do to save our lives.

In the nineteenth century, foot jugglers, or antipodists, began juggling immense playing cards, parasols, tables, and dummy figures. They even used human beings instead of inanimate objects in their acts.

Richard Risley Carlisle, an American born in 1814, combined juggling with acrobatics. He had a troupe of Oriental tumblers lie on their backs. Carlisle then juggled the lightest members of the troupe in a fast and exciting routine. People flocked to see the Carlisle act, and soon there were many imitators in American and European circuses.

Emil Otto Braun, who was born in Posen, Poland, in 1859, started his circus career as an acrobat until a fall from a trapeze kept him in bed for several weeks. For lack of anything else to do, he taught himself juggling and soon discovered that he liked that circus skill best of all. An acrobatic clown, Cinquevalli, coached Braun in some of the finer juggling techniques, and Braun adopted the stage name Cinquevalli, in honor of his teacher.

Cinquevalli has been described as a combination of juggler, comic, showman, and strongman. When in the circus arena, he wore a curly wig that sparkled with golden glitter and a costume deco-

49

Cannonball juggler in the Ringling Bros. and Barnum & Bailey Circus, 1912.

WORLD'S GREATEST SHOWS

UMAN TOP AND MODERN HERCULES.

51

rated with sequins. One of his favorite tricks was to juggle a lump of sugar, a teapot, a cup, and a saucer. After making these items fly gracefully through the air, he then dropped the sugar into the cup and dropped the cup on the saucer, while he simultaneously poured tea out of the pot into the cup.

If you think that sounds difficult, just imagine another Cinquevalli routine. He held a blowpipe containing a dart in his left hand while he juggled a sharp knife, a fork, and a turnip with his right hand. For the act's finale, he puffed on the blowpipe so that the dart pierced the turnip high in the air at the exact moment the fork's tines stuck into the vegetable. He impaled all three objects on the knife as they dropped back into his hands!

Needless to say, audiences loved Cinquevalli. He soon became the star of the circus ring. He arrived in England in 1885 and became a naturalized British subject in 1893. But during World War I the circus spectators who had cheered him for many years suddenly remembered his German-Polish background. Love turned to hatred, and their applause to jeers. Cinquevalli was forced to leave the circus in disgrace. One of the greatest jugglers in history soon died of a broken heart.

The man who was regarded as superior even to Cinquevalli was Enrico Rastelli. One story says that he was born in northern Italy, at Bergamo in Lombardy, in 1897; another, that he was born in Siberia in 1896 while his circus family was touring Russia. Enrico Rastelli's father and grandfather were

MR. VILALLAVE

AND Family, return their sincere thanks to the citizens of Portland, for the liberal patronage and evident favor accorded to them on their first appearance, and would respectfully inform them, that they will make their *second appearance*, TO MORROW EVENING, August 1.

The Performance will commence with GRAND DANCES of the TIGHT ROPE, by Master and Miss Vilallave.

FANCY DANCE by Madame Vilallave, on the Rope.

TURKISH DANCE by Mr. Vilallave.

The Grand Double Dance by Mr. V. and the Chinese on the Rope.

Master and Miss V. will dance LA GAVOTTE on the Stage.

HERCULEAN & AGILE FEATS, by Mr. Vilallave, the Chinese, Master & Miss Vilallave.

GROUND & LOFTY TUMBLING, &c. &c.

The whole to conclude with the elegant imitation of CHINESE FIRE WORKS.

Admittance to boxes 50 cts.—Other seats 25 cts.—Children with their parents to the boxes, half price.

☞ The next performance will take place on Friday evening next

Mr. Vilallave, juggler with Vilallave's Circus.

jugglers, and it has been reported that Rastelli's ancestors had been jugglers as far back as the eighth generation. At one time his father owned a small European circus in which his mother performed as a trapeze artiste.

Enrico Rastelli worked with his mother in an aerial act, while his father juggled on horseback in the ring. Jugglers were poorly paid, so the elder Rastelli insisted that his son become an aerialist instead of a juggler. "You will lead a better life," said Enrico's father.

But the boy was already in love with juggling. Despite his father's orders, Enrico Rastelli started to practice juggling in secret when he was only eight years old. After several years, he was able to juggle seven balls. When a Japanese troupe came to perform in the circus, Rastelli learned foot juggling and the use of a mouth stick. The famous juggler Takashima was one of his teachers.

When his father discovered how expert the boy had become, he changed his earlier attitude. "If you can juggle that well now, you'll probably be able to do wonderful things with more time for practice," said the elder Rastelli. "I guess you'll have to become a juggler after all."

Enrico Rastelli practiced night and day. He often juggled twelve hours a day and seldom less than six. It is said that he talked with other performers and even conducted his business affairs while juggling. He loved the art of juggling and his

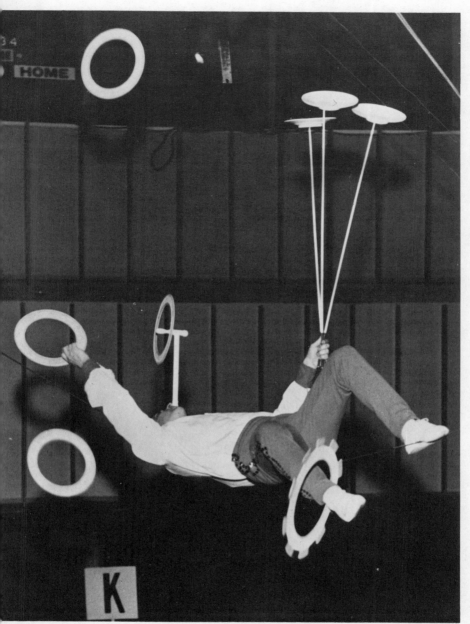

Bojilov, one of the world's few slack-wire jugglers, performs feats never even attempted by jugglers who have both feet on the ground.

love was clearly reflected in the marvelous feats he accomplished.

Enrico threw and caught a large child's rubber ball, six to twelve inches in diameter, bouncing it off various parts of his body. He began the practice of throwing a ball into a circus audience, having a spectator throw it back, and catching the ball on a stick held in his mouth. Many other circus jugglers have since adopted the trick. Rastelli also used a football and a soccer ball in his act. He dazzled professional players and fans by holding lengthy conversations while bouncing the two balls off his forehead.

Small rubber balls, sticks, and plates were Rastelli specialties when he performed at the Hippodrome in New York in 1923. When he returned to Europe shortly thereafter, he cut his lip on a mouthpiece he used in his act and became ill with an infection. The "greatest juggler in the world" died when he was only thirty-five years old, at the height of his circus career.

Artists such as the Ringling Bros. and Barnum & Bailey Circus salon juggler Felix Adanos are magnificent and talented, but they have never equaled the extraordinary feats of Enrico Rastelli. The little boy who was forced to rehearse in secret grew up to become the best juggler the stage or circus arena has ever known. His artistry may never be surpassed. Or someone new, quite possibly you, may become the world's next great juggler-entertainer.